Where Can I Find *God?*

HELEN DOSS

Drawings by Frank Aloise

ABINGDON PRESS

Nashville   New York

Copyright © 1968 by Abingdon Press
All Rights Reserved
Printed in the United States of America
Library of Congress Catalog Card Number 68:10704

PZ7
. D72w
1968

To
DAVID E. EITZEN
who teaches about God
within and among us,
whose own life reveals a continual
awareness of God's presence

*". . . seek God . . . he is not far
from each one of us, for in him
we live and move and have our
being . . ." Acts 17:27-29.*

I can't see God.
Not the way I can *see* my father or my mother,
   my sister or my brother.
I just can't see God the way I can see my friends.
I can *see* people,
      and *touch* people,
         and *hear* people.
I can bump into people—and there they are!
It isn't that way with God.

I can't see God or touch him.
I can't hear his voice out loud,
    not the way I can hear people talking.
I can't bump into God—not with my body,
    not the way I do with people.
But I know that God *is*.

I know God made our radiant sun
    and our silver-lighted moon.
God made meteors, blazing through our upper air;
    Comets, glowing-tailed, which swivel round our sun;
    and the circling, circling planets.
God made all the glistening stars that I can see and count,
    and out beyond *that,*
        farther than *anyone* knows,
            farther than I can think—
Thousands . . . and millions . . . and billions of stars.
This is God's work.
God is out there. *Right now, God is out there.*
I know that.

People can think up rockets and make them.
People can blast off rockets
    to explore the nearby outer space.
People can build giant telescopes
    to peer into the mysterious universe.
But—people cannot *make* a universe.

And nothing so wonder-*full* could just create itself.
Gigantic, whirling galaxies of stars,
    the nearby blazing star we call our sun,
        the circling planets with little moons,
            our molten-cored, rock-crusted earth—
God made it all. God is there, the maker of it all.

A tree stretches leafy green fingers to the sky;
    up the trunk streams a highway of busy ants.
In a hollow below, a whisker-twitching rabbit
    cuddles her jumpy, skittery babies.
I think, *God made you!*

My eyes follow a hawk as he swoops
    in the blue bowl of the sky.
I think, *God made you. God soars on your wings too.*
God made the trees, the bugs, the rabbits, the birds;
    he made all the flying, swimming,
        crawling, walking
            creatures of this earth.

My dog looks up at me, with brown loving eyes.
There is something of God
        in the way I care about my dog,
            and in the way my dog cares about me.
There is something of God in all his creatures.

When a friend takes my hand and smiles at me,
    I feel God is right here.
When somebody takes time and *listens* to me,
        listens with his eyes and the whole of him,
        when he listens to me as if he *likes* me—
God is right here with us.
When I am with people and they like each other,
When they care about what is happening to each other,
        when they *really* care—
        God is there.
Yes, I can feel God right here among us!

When I think nice things about my mother and father,
    a lovely warm feeling begins to grow inside me,
    and then—I know God is right *here.*
Parents aren't perfect. Parents are people—
    they have feelings just like anyone else,
    and sometimes they make mistakes.
I'm not perfect either.
    Nobody is.
    I often make mistakes or have hurt feelings.
But—when my parents love me anyway, just the way I am,
    and I love my parents anyway, just the way they are,
    I know God is right here.
God is right here among us.

When I think of people who have felt close to God,
    then I feel close to God too.
Moses felt close to God, leading his people to freedom.
And King David! Even when he was young,
    watching over his sheep, David felt close to God.
When Jeremiah's enemies jailed him in a deep, dark well—
    even then Jeremiah felt God's nearness.
These people in the Bible were all *real* people.
They lived, and ate, and worried, just like me,
    and they all tried to learn more about God.
What *they* learned helps *me*.

I listen to the Bible stories. I think about
    the teachings of the man called Jesus,
    and I feel closer to God.
When I read about Jesus, I think:
    There was God within a man.
There was God, part of the man named Jesus.
There was God, showing us something of himself.

Sometimes I feel closest to God when I am all alone.
When a good idea comes to me, I think:
    God is right here, ready to help me.
Sometimes I do something good for someone
    without really thinking about it,
    just because it feels like the right thing to do—
And then I know it is God, inside me, close to me,
    helping me.

Sometimes I start to do something I really shouldn't,
    and something inside me says No!
And then I know it is God, inside me, helping me,
    close to me.
Yes, sometimes I feel closest to God when I am
    all alone.

I can't see God—
      not the way I can see my father or my mother,
      or a brother or a sister or a friend.
I can't hear God or feel him with my hands,

But I can see him in the night sky at work in his
      wonder-filled universe.
I can feel God's warming sunshine,
      and feel the wetness of the rain.

I can see something of God in all the animals he created,
 in the fish of the sea,
 in the birds of the sky.

I can see God and feel his presence among
 all his people,
 all his different kinds of people.

Perhaps you can say I do bump into God,
        everywhere I go, any way I turn.
Even when I'm alone, all by myself
        with my eyes closed,
        God is right here.
I can feel God here—inside of me, part of *me*.
Where can I find God?
        Inside of me,
        all around me,
        and far, far beyond me—
Everywhere, *everywhere,* there is God.